The

WORDS

of

RUMI

THIS BOOK BELONGS TO

OTHER WORKS BY RASOUL SHAMS
Published by the Rumi Poetry Club

Rumi: The Art of Loving

Rumi Essays: On the Life, Poetry, and Vision of the Greatest Persian Sufi Poet

THE WORDS OF RUMI

Celebrating a Year of Inspiration
with
Jalâluddin Rumi

Selected and translated by
Rasoul Shams

RUMI PUBLICATIONS
an imprint of
RUMI POETRY CLUB
2017

THE WORDS OF RUMI:
CELEBRATING A YEAR OF INSPIRATION

Jalâluddin Rumi
Selected and translated by Rasoul Shams

Copyright © 2017 Rumi Poetry Club
All rights reserved.
No part of this book may be published, reproduced, translated or transmitted in any form or by any means without written permission of the publisher, except in the case of brief quotations (with citation) embodied in critical articles and reviews.

ISBN-13: 978-0-9850568-3-4
ISBN-10: 0-9850568-3-5

Library of Congress Control Number: 2017957535

First Published in 2017
Rumi Poetry Club
P.O. Box 521376
Salt Lake City, UT 84152-1376
Email: info@rumipoetryclub.com
Website: www.rumipoetryclub.com
Facebook: www.facebook.com/rumipoetryclub

Cover painting by Setsuko Yoshida

Printed in the United States of America

Rumi's Advice

In generosity and helping others,
be like the river.
In compassion and grace,
be like the sun.
In concealing others' faults,
be like the night.
In anger and rage,
be as if you are dead.
In modesty and humility,
be like the soil.
In patience and tolerance,
be like the sea.
In life,
be yourself, be as you appear to the sight.

An oral tradition attributed to Rumi

Contents

Preface			9
January	I	Words	17
February	II	Quest	22
March	III	Awakening	28
April	IV	Life	34
May	V	Mind	39
June	VI	Love	45
July	VII	Happiness	50
August	VIII	Heart	56
September	IX	Universe	62
October	X	Union	69
November	XI	Prayers	76
December	XII	Silence	83
Rumi's Proverbs			88
Rumi's Last Will			92
The Reed Flute's Song			93
Sources and Notes			95
Acknowledgments			100

PREFACE

"I write this book for love of your love."
                                    St. Augustine

We celebrate "Years" and "Anniversaries" of all kinds. Let's celebrate a whole "Year of Inspiration" for ourselves, in the solitude of our hearts. The word "inspiration" is indeed beautiful. It means "breathing in;" it is intimately related with life itself. Although this word entered the English language in the fourteenth century, its meaning can be traced back to the story of humankind's creation in which God breathed from His/Her own spirit into the human body, which was made from earth. Indeed, God breathes into us each and every moment. Inspiration means life, spirit, and creativity; it is the breathing of the soul and vivid pulsation of the heart. All great discoveries, inventions, ideas, actions, and life transformations have begun with inspiration.

Many years ago, I read a small book entitled *The Words of Gandhi*. This book was an anthology of Gandhi's sayings selected by Sir Richard Attenborough (director of the film *Gandhi*). Even though I had read a few other books about Mahatma Gandhi, I found that small book of quotations quite inspirational, and have kept it in my personal library. Over the past three decades, as I have voyaged through the ocean of Rumi's poetry, I have noted phrases and short poems that have inspired me profoundly. I am sure many readers of Rumi have similar experiences and impressions. Recently, I decided to compile a selection of Rumi quotes for the benefit of those who would perhaps like to see the essential teachings of Rumi in brief passages in a single, handy volume – hence this book.

Jalâluddin Rumi was a great Persian Sufi poet; he was born in 1207 in the city of Balkh in present-day Afghanistan, and died in 1273 in the city of Konya (where he lived most of his life) in present-day Turkey. He was born and died on a Sunday – a beautiful and fitting symbol for his poetry of light and love. At age 37, in the market of sugar-sellers in Konya, Rumi happened to meet a wandering dervish, Shams ("Sun") of Tabriz (a city in northwest Iran). His friendship and conversations with Shams transformed Rumi's life from that of a scholar and preacher to one of a mystic and poet of love. In my previous book, *Rumi Essays: On the Life, Work, and Vision of the Greatest Persian Sufi Poet* (2016), there is a fairly comprehensive biography of Rumi, and that information is not repeated here for the sake of space.

Why should we listen to the words of a man who lived eight centuries ago? Our basic needs and life problems are the same today as they were centuries ago: We all long to understand who we are and what this world is about; we all want to be happy and live in peace both mentally and socially; and we all inherently want to do good work and live a meaningful life. Rumi has precious teachings to offer us. His words matter because of his rare personality too. He embodied the elegant sensitivity and skillful language of a poet, the vast knowledge and deep thought of a philosopher, the insight and metaphysical vision of a mystic, and the loving heart of a saint. Each of these fields would consume a person's whole life, but under certain circumstances of his time as well as by his own effort, Rumi integrated these qualities in his person and life journey. That is why his poems and words reach us centuries later, and are sweet to our ears and lips, no matter in which language we read them. Indeed, Rumi is one of the most widely read poets in English today and ranks amongst Shakespeare, William Blake, Walt Whitman, Emily Dickinson and other luminaries in the constellation of English literature.

I first encountered Rumi's poems as a school boy growing up in Iran. Some of his poems were easy to understand, but many of his verses and metaphors were hard to grasp for us young students. Nevertheless, we were instructed to memorize them for our Persian literature classes. I remember our teacher once said: "You should not be discouraged by the poet's apparently difficult expressions because he composed these verses not when he was a young boy, as you are today, but when he was in the middle of his life, or as he himself says when he was mature and cooked. As you grow older, these poems will come back to you in your life, and you will appreciate them better." How true this statement has proven to be! Since leaving Iran, I have lived in India, Japan and the USA for nearly four decades, and all through these years, Rumi's poetry has been a source of insight, strength, inspiration, and guidance.

Professor Edward Browne (1862-1926) of Cambridge University once remarked that Rumi's "mystical *Mathnawi* deserves to rank amongst the great poems of all time." This anthology of Rumi you hold in your hands is largely based on the *Masnavi* (pronounced *Mathnawi* in Arabic) – a work of 26,000 verses which Rumi composed during the last twelve years of his life. The *Mansavi* is a collection in six volumes of parables and stories in verse intertwined with Rumi's teachings and aphorisms. For this volume, I have selected and translated from Rumi's aphorisms, and have categorized those under twelve broad themes: *Words, Quest, Awakening, Life, Mind, Love, Happiness, Heart, Universe, Union, Prayers,* and *Silence*.

This book is thus divided into twelve topical chapters – each chapter for a month of the year. I have included 21 aphorisms (rather than 30 or 31) in each chapter so that the reader can follow at his or her own pace and has some days off to digest and reflect on the verses and teachings; everything in moderation, even meditation. There are various ways to use this book. Those who have already read Rumi extensively may read this anthology at random to refresh and deepen their learning and understanding. One may also read the entire book in a few days, and revisit it at other times. Or the reader can use the reading of this book as a year-long spiritual journey – one chapter a month as specified in the book. In this case, I suggest reading each aphorism three times – silently, loud out, and then again silently. I would also recommend to keep a journal, write each quote in the journal, contemplate on it, and finally write in brief sentences your own impression as the phrase speaks to your life and soul.

In short, read, contemplate, and write in a journal. Moreover, read the meanings of words in each phrase in their context. A given word may have different meanings depending on its context and cannot be generalized beyond its scope. Writing in a journal can be helpful in this regard. As the editor and translator of this volume, I do not expect that all readers will have the same impressions and usage for all of the aphorisms in the book simply because we all come from different backgrounds and have different experiences and challenges. So it is fine if some phrases appeal to you more than the others; keep reading and let the book lead you to yourself. I should also add a note here: Third-person pronouns in Persian are gender neutral; there is no he or she ("oo," pronounced as in "ooze," implies both he and she); God has no gender, either. I had to pick he or she in the translation of Rumi's poems in this volume, but you are welcome to change them.

I have also added a chapter on Rumi's poetic phrases which have been used as proverbs in the Persian language for centuries. Finally, I have translated Rumi's Last Will which contains his final advice to his disciples and family. These two chapters give a different flavor to this collection of Rumi's words. Enjoy them as well.

All of Rumi's quotations in this book are my translations directly from the Persian language in which he wrote his books. Translating classical literature, particularly poetry with its subtleties, into a modern language is not an easy task. Nonetheless, I have endeavored that Rumi speak for himself in plain English. For those readers with scholarly view and curiosity the sources of the quotations are given at the end of the book. I hope the readers will find in these pages a flavor of Rumi's thought and message, and will find Rumi's words inspirational and useful in their life journeys.

In *The Way of Passion: A Celebration of Rumi*, Andrew Harvey writes, "Rumi has seen right into the volcano of creation." This line beautifully captures what many of Rumi's avid readers have also felt about the liberating power and vivid imagery of his poetry. As Harvey mentions, because Rumi had seen "this vast dance of fire – worlds arising and falling back," he speaks of the "immense and fabulous extravagance of the soul." And remember that "out of the soul is being created the oceanic trenches, supernovas, wars, madness, ecstasy, everything." I hope in this book Rumi's soul speaks to your soul.

***

E. B. White once remarked, "Remember that writing is translation, and the opus to be translated is yourself." Likewise, in one of his poems, Rumi says:

> *I bring messages from the Sun.*
> *I am the Sun's translator.*
> *And this is how I do it:*
> *Secretly, I ask the Sun,*
> *Then I answer your question.*

I wrote these Rumi aphorisms initially for myself, and I am delighted to share them in the form of this book. Thank you for bringing presence and life to these words!

Rasoul Shams,
Salt Lake City
September 30, 2017
(Rumi's birthday)

Come, come again whoever you are,
come here.
Atheist, pagan, idol worshipper –
whatever you are, come,
Our home is the home of
never losing hope.
Even if you have broken
your repentance and vows
a hundred times,
come, come again.

A famous Sufi poem inscribed in
Rumi's shrine in Konya

*Words, like Nature, half reveal
And half conceal the Soul within.*

Alfred Lord Tennyson

I. WORDS
January

The *Gospel of John* begins with a beautiful phrase: "In the beginning was the Word (*logos*)." Similarly, the *Qurân* (II: 117) says: "When God wishes to create something, He simply says, 'Be' (*kun*) and it *is*". The Word is thus a symbol of manifestation and creation. Human thought and reasoning (*logic*) are also related to words; language plays an important role in our thinking and feeling. Of course, language and words have limitations, and spiritual teachers emphasize that truth, beauty, joy, goodness and other features of spirituality should be experienced directly; words, whether written or spoken, cannot describe the experiences of the heart, let alone replace them. Nevertheless, when words come from our higher consciousness, that is, from deeper parts of our hearts, they make an opening into the infinite realm of meaning and the Spirit. Words, when properly spoken and heard, take us on a journey to a world beyond words. And in this regard, Rumi is a master poet. Listening to poetry, stories and music is an important practice in Sufism. Let's begin our spiritual journey in this book with meditations on words and listening.

★ I.1 ★

Love wishes these words to be released.

★ I.2 ★

Seek spiritual knowledge, awareness,
and enlightenment directly from God,
not from books, lectures, or word of mouth.

★ I.3 ★

Any voice that uplifts your spirit
is a call from the highest plane.
And any voice that instigates greed in you
is the howl of the wolf preparing to tear up lives.

★ I.4 ★

Words and songs arise from the mind.
Yet, you do not know where the sea of the mind lies.
Nonetheless, if you see words surfing on tender and
pleasant waves towards you, rest assured they arise
from a noble, generous sea.

★ I.5 ★

Words are like a container, and meaning is
like water in it. The ocean of meaning is
the mother of all books, and *that* resides with God.

★ I.6 ★

Meaning is a treasure hidden in the sands of words.

✶ I.7 ✶
When listening deepens, it becomes seeing.

✶ I.8 ✶
A listening ear becomes an eye,
just as a stone through love becomes a gem.

✶ I.9 ✶
When someone listens with thirst and a spirit of
seeking, the speaker, even if worn down,
becomes an eloquent and a fine orator.

✶ I.10 ✶
Everything that is elegant and beautiful is
made for the eye of the person who *sees*.
Song and melody is never offered to an ear
that is senseless and deaf.

✶ I.11 ✶
Discard the donkey ear if you have one,
and use your ear of inner listening because
the donkey ear cannot comprehend the Word.

✶ I.12 ✶
Water talks; earth talks. But they are heard
only by the people whose hearts are open.

✶ I.13 ✶
To learn how to speak one must listen first.
Try to speak to others through listening to them.

★ I.14 ★

The best words need not be numerous and verbose.
The best words are those that truly help us.

★ I.15 ★

When words are too much decorated,
>their purpose is easily forgotten.

★ I.16 ★

Words and names can actually be pitfalls and traps
on the spiritual path. Seek fresh words that pour out
>from the Water of Life.

★ I.17 ★

Wisdom is like rain; it is infinite at the source,
but it comes down in appropriate amounts –
in winter, spring, summer and autumn –
more or less according to the season.

★ I.18 ★

One, who is calm and aware,
comprehends a great deal from so little,
many things from one thing,
and volumes of books from a single line.

★ I.19 ★

Words are shadows of reality; they branch from
reality and are thus subordinate to it.
If the shadow can be attractive,
imagine how much more the reality can be.

⋆ I.20 ⋆

The Voice that is the source of every song and cry
is the genuine Voice; the rest are mere echoes.
All people – whether speaking Turkish, Kurdish,
Persian or Arabic – understand that Voice,
even without ears or moving lips.
For that matter, wood and stone also
understand that Voice.

⋆ I.21 ⋆

The wisdom seeker eventually becomes
        the source of wisdom and
is relieved from secondary knowledge and
        the means of acquiring such knowledge.

II. Quest

February

Although the terms "question" and "quest" have the same Latin root, *quaerere*, and both appeared in English in the fourteenth century, they have entirely different meanings. A question (or a query) is an intellectual inquiry of some specific thing; it may even imply doubt and dispute. Once we find the answer (oftentimes given to us by others), we understand it intellectually, and that satisfies our curiosity (or we continue to ask related questions). Quest, on the other hand, is a search with our total being; it is an inner, individual experience of journeying in a land uncharted by us, no matter how many others have gone that path before. Questions are rooted in the rational mind and form the basis of the scientific method; they are conversations in language and logic. Quest belongs to the realm of the heart; it is a relationship with a mystery – the *Logos* – not to solve it but to be absorbed in it. Quest envelopes pains of separation, pathways of pilgrimage, and passions of union, ecstasy and tranquility. Rumi says that a genuine quest begins with lament and longing, much like a crying reed flute.

II.1

Listen to the reed-flute, how it laments.
It narrates the story of separation:

> *Ever since I was cut from the reed-bed,*
> *men and women have cried in my lament.*
> *I seek out a heart shredded into pieces*
> *by separation, then only can I describe*
> *the pain of this longing.*
> *Whoever is left far from his origin*
> *seeks to return to the days of union.*

II.2

It is the longing for You that fans my urge.
It is the attraction of Truth
that draws the seeker along the path.
With no wind, how can the dust rise up?
Without the sea, how can the boat sail?

II.3

Just as the thirsty look for water,
water seeks the thirsty all over the world.

II.4

There is no lover seeking union
without a beloved searching for him, too.
A single hand's clapping cannot produce sound
without being accompanied by the other hand.
A thirsty person cries for fresh water;
while the water is groaning: Who is the drinker?
We belong to Water, and Water belongs to us.

⋆ II.5 ⋆

Do not seek water; seek thirst.
Then fresh water will gush forth
                              from above and below.

⋆ II.6 ⋆

If you desire Light, you should prepare yourself
                          to deserve Light.

⋆ II.7 ⋆

If you desire tears of longing,
      show kindness to one who sheds tears.
If you desire God's kindness,
      show kindness to the weak.

⋆ II.8 ⋆

Whether your pace is slow or fast,
as long as you are a seeker you will find.

⋆ II.9 ⋆

Redouble your effort and always blend your search
with dance and joy, for the search itself
will guide you on the good path.

⋆ II.10 ⋆

Your inner feeling of having faults and doubt
is actually God's mercy in order to guide you.

★ II.11 ★

Wherever your search for God takes you,
                                       marvel not.
Don't gaze at your weaknesses;
                         focus on your quest.
It is God who put this search in your heart.
Every seeker deserves
                  what he or she searches for.
Strive to intensify your quest.
Then your heart will come out of
                           this dark worldly well.

★ II.12 ★

When God wishes to help us,
        he urges us to weep and lament.
The eye that sheds tears in search of God
                         is, indeed, blessed.
And the heart that burns for God
                    comes out victorious.

★ II.13 ★

Wherever water flows the ground becomes green.
Wherever tears fall the Divine mercy grows.
Let your eyes weep like a waterwheel:
Healing herbs will grow from the soil of your soul.

★ II.14 ★

At the end of every weeping comes joy and laughter.
Blessed is the one who gazes at the ending;
that person is the true devotee.

★ II.15 ★

My entire mind revolves around one thing:
                              Longing for you.
This 'I' should die before your graceful presence.

★ II.16 ★

The worldly sense is
                the ladder to this world.
The spiritual sense is
                the ladder to heaven.
Seek the health of your bodily sense
                from a physician,
and the health of your spiritual sense
                only from the Beloved.

★ II.17 ★

Let painstaking work melt away
your ungrateful rebellious mood.
The work will provide a shade – a sanctuary,
in which you will enjoy being with the Beloved
as if you have found a rare treasure.

★ II.18 ★

If the bird in the cage does not seek freedom,
it simply demonstrates its ignorance.
Those great souls and prophets,
who escaped from the worldly cage,
are indeed qualified guides for others.

★ II.19 ★

Every prophet and saint has a path.
But they all are one
as they lead to the same Truth of God.

★ II.20 ★

The seeker eventually becomes the finder,
for God's shade protects the devotee on her path

★ II.21 ★

If the seeker's legs fail,
>   God bestows her a pair of wings.
He opens a door to salvation
>   even in the depths of a dark well.

III. AWAKENING
March

There is a saying attributed to the seventh-century Muslim leader and sage, Ali: "People are asleep; when they die they wake up." What does this mean? Those who have set their eyes on life after death interpret this saying to mean that this life is a dream; the after-life is real. Sufis, however, emphasize that the purpose of human life is not to sleepwalk in this world and then die; we should live and enjoy this life mindfully, and this is possible through the death of the ever-desiring and ever-dreaming selfish ego. In Indian terminology, living in sleep is called *maya* (illusion) while the person who is awakened is known as a *buddha*. Spiritual awakening is usually likened to illumination – going from darkness to light. As the spiritual sun rises from the orient of our hearts and our spiritual eyes open, we can see the reality as well as the illusion of self, life, and the world. We can then encounter God, not after death, but in each moment of life: We can see God in action in all of creation as well as in our own hearts. Spiritual awakening has been called a "second birth" that takes place after the "extinction" of the fire of ego – a stage called *nirvana* in Buddhism and *fanâ* in Sufism.

✶ III.1 ✶

At the time of death the rich man realizes that
        he owns no wealth.
And the clever man realizes that
        he wasn't really clever.

✶ III.2 ✶

The more awake one is to this mundane world
the more asleep he is to the spiritual world.

✶ III.3 ✶

When the soul is not awake to God and Reality,
it is like possessing proper eyes but living in a prison.

✶ III.4 ✶

Do not be surprised that the soul does not remember its original home, for this world is like a sleep and puts a veil on mysterious reality just as the clouds cover the stars.

✶ III.5 ✶

Holding a blue glass before your eyes,
the whole world will look blue to you.

✶ III.6 ✶

The essence of all knowledge is
to know yourself in the ultimate reckoning.
You may know the principles of your religion very well. Now look at the Root Principle within yourself: Is it functioning well?

★ III.7 ★

The earth and the heavens are like an apple –
> manifested on the tree of God's power.

And we are like a worm in the apple –
> unaware of the tree or of the Gardener.

There is another worm in the apple too.
> It is the spirit –
> exalted and extending beyond the apple.

★ III.8 ★

An empty, sealed jar, even if immersed in turbulent water, will float because its interior is filled with air. Likewise, when your inner space is filled with the Spirit, you can rest peacefully on the waves of the world's turbulent waters.

★ III.9 ★

This world, which has no existence of its own,
> looks like concrete being,

while the realm of real existence is hidden.
The world we see is like the dust in the wind –
> displaying distorted images and invisibility.

★ III.10 ★

If God permits your eyes to see in His light,
a hundred more worlds will come to your sight.

✶ III.11 ✶

We hit each other in life like the boats
on the sea dashing against each other.
Reality is like the bright, clear water,
but our eyes do not see it clearly.
O you who have gone into sleep
    in the boat of your body!
You have seen water in your dream.
Now behold the water of water –
    the reality of this sea and your boat.

✶ III.12 ✶

With no light outside we cannot see colors.
So it is with the colors of inner vision.
The outer light comes from the sun and stars.
The inner light is a reflection of the Light of lights.
The light of the light of the eye
    is the light of the heart.
Indeed, the true light of our vision
    is an outcome of the light of the heart.
The light that illuminates the heart
    is the pure Divine Light.

✶ III.13 ✶

Even though the wall may cast a long shadow,
the shadow eventually returns to the wall.
This world is a mountain, and our action
is like shouting on the mountain;
the echo comes back to us.

★ III.14 ★

If you dig a well, out of injustice, for others to fall in,
indeed you have dug a trap for yourself.

★ III.15 ★

This has been reported from the Prophet:
Faithful humans are like mirrors to one another.

★ III.16 ★

To me, one hundred years or one hour are the same.
For I am not concerned with the length or shortness
of time. Being long or short is for physical objects,
not for the ever-present Spirit.

★ III.17 ★

Now that we have become aware of the Spirit,
a seal has been put on our lips so that
the secrets of the unseen realm are not revealed,
and this world of pleasure and business keeps going.

★ III.18 ★

We are like the harp; You are playing us.
This lamenting sound is not ours;
      it comes from You.
We are like the reed-flute;
      the music in us is from You.
We are like the mountain echoing Your voice.
Or like the chess pieces in play;
      our victories and defeats are really from You.

III.19

How can we say we exist
>   while You are the Soul of our souls?
How can we say we exist
>   when You have filled us all the time?
We and our 'I's are really non-existent.
You are the real being, but appear as non-being,
for you are manifested in the perishable phenomena.

III.20

The Light of God purifies and beautifies
>   the light of our physical senses.
This is the meaning of the saying "*Light upon light*."
Let the Light guide your senses;
>   it is a good companion.

III.21

When the selfish ego dies,
you become alive and aware in the presence of God,
and the secrets of Reality come to your lips.

IV. Life
April

This much is certain – to the materialist or otherwise: We live in this world. But "this world" is a double-edged sword. On the one hand, being hooked to the "mundane world" and "pleasures of the flesh" is life imprisonment for the soul who knows another life. On the other hand, the world is God's creation brimming with beauty and wonder, and this life is a gift of joy, consciousness, and creativity. Spiritual life is liberation from the worldly attachments, such as wealth at any cost, fame to boost our ego, and power to dominate others. Spiritual life means living by the spirit of truth, beauty, goodness, and joy in the heart.

What is this world? Our answer to this question defines our relationships and the quality and meaning of our lives. Life, particularly in the contemporary world, can be so overwhelming and full of distractions and illusions. How to "be in the world but not of the world"? This is a challenge for all of us, always and everywhere. Rumi offers some suggestions from his own findings.

IV.1

In my entire quest in this world, I have not seen anything more worthy than good character.

IV.2

This world is a prison, and we are prisoners.
Dig a hole and liberate yourself.
What does "this world" mean?
It does not mean your clothes, food or spouse.
It means to be forgetful of God.

IV.3

Prophet Muhammad said:
> *Righteous wealth is a blessing.*

This is the wealth you carry on the good path.
Wealth is like sea water:
Beneath the boat, water is life support,
but water filling the boat is its death.

IV.4

Rigidity, harshness, and prejudice are all signs of spiritual immaturity.
And as long as one's soul is unripe, his life,
like that of an embryo, is blood drinking.

⋆ IV.5 ⋆

The smell of arrogance and greed,
        like the smell of an onion,
is readily felt from people's talk.

⋆ IV.6 ⋆

When God wants to shame someone,
the person itches to offend good people.
And when God wants to cover someone's faults,
the person does not meddle with people's faults.

⋆ IV.7 ⋆

If your anger spreads fire to the hearts of people,
you become the very source of hell fire.

⋆ IV.8 ⋆

Hatred and malice, including yours, are rooted in
hell, and they are against the spirit of religion.

⋆ IV.9 ⋆

Hell is a dragon with seven heads.
It builds a snare whose bait is greed.
Tear down that snare and burn that bait.
Open new doors to the house of your life.

⋆ IV.10 ⋆

Whoever observes his own faults
                  before others point them out
      will always strive to correct his character.
The reason people speak of each other's faults
is that they do not pay attention to their own.

✶ IV.11 ✶

You see evil things in others,
but not clearly in yourself.
If you actually see those things in yourself,
you will become your own worst enemy.

✶ IV.12 ✶

To abandon lust and selfish pleasure is
                to be generous to yourself,
for whoever is drowned in lust does not rise up.

✶ IV.13 ✶

The worldly man is indeed poor and full of fears.
He owns nothing and yet has dread of thieves.
He comes to this world naked and departs naked.
But the anxiety of thieves torments for his entire life.

✶ IV.14 ✶

All sorrows and worries within our chests
are vapors that arise from the burning of our lives.
They are the dust of our desire-winds.

✶ IV.15 ✶

Do not exhaust yourself to accomplish worldly
affairs. Devote your effort to the spiritual path.
Otherwise, in the end, you will depart life
unfulfilled. Your affairs will remain unfinished;
                your bread unbaked.

✶ IV.16 ✶

For your soul, feeling pain and grief is far better than
having a world empire, because in pain
you call to God in the solitude of your heart.

✶ IV.17 ✶

Refresh your faith, not merely with the words of the
tongue but within you, for that is also where you
replenish your selfish desires. As long as your greed
is kept fresh, your faith and trust will not grow.

✶ IV.18 ✶

Worrisome thoughts result from recollection of the
past. Past and future are both curtains of separation
from God. Cast fire on both of them.
How long will you be tormented by
> the non-existent past or future?

✶ IV.19 ✶

Each person is created with a talent to do a certain
work, and the love of that work lies in the person's
heart.

✶ IV.20 ✶

Don't keep saying, "Tomorrow, tomorrow."
Those "tomorrows" have already passed.
Now take care that this day does not pass unfulfilled.

✶ IV.21 ✶

Good people die too, but their good deeds remain.

V. Mind
May

Mind, like the word "world" discussed in the previous chapter, has two opposite contexts and connotations. On the one hand, "mind" means a heavy occupation with thoughts and worries – with regrets of the past or anxiety of the future. This kind of mind is not desirable because it prevents us from living in the moment, from enjoying life and from seeing the reality and beauty of the world; it may even have harmful effects on our health and wellbeing. The small self-centered mind reduces us to a suffering creature, no matter where we are or what we do. That is why meditation is said to be a state of no-mind. On the other hand, "mind" as in mindfulness or good mind, implies a consciousness rooted in reality, in the present moment, and in the heart. Spiritual teachers invite us to embrace this kind of mind because it is the source of real knowing, joy, compassion, and creativity. To go from Mind I to Mind II, we need training, practice, and conversation with friends who have seen both minds. In this chapter, Rumi offers such a conversation and friendship.

⋆ V.1 ⋆

People are captives of their own thoughts.
That is why their hearts are dis-eased
                and exhausted by sorrows.

⋆ V.2 ⋆

The legs of argumentative people are made of wood.
Walking with wooden legs can be quite shaky.

⋆ V.3 ⋆

Real knowledge has two wings, opinion only one.
Because of this shortcoming, an opinionated person
does not fly to the heights of the tree of knowledge.

⋆ V.4 ⋆

There are many scholars who are devoid of real
wisdom because their minds are merely filled with
information;
      because they are not lovers.

⋆ V.5 ⋆

There are people who know a hundred thousand bits
of information from the sciences, but alas,
                they do not know themselves.
They may know the property of every substance,
but when it comes to their own Substance,
                they remain ignorant.

✶ V.6 ✶

If your thoughts are roses,
                      you are a rose garden.
If your thoughts are thorns,
               you are fuel for the fire stove.

✶ V.7 ✶

When selfishness and negativity enter your mind,
your friend's virtues are eclipsed.
       Because a hundred veils block the way
       between your heart and your eye.

✶ V.8 ✶

One wise mind plus another doubles wisdom:
       Light then increases, and the right path
       comes to sight.
One selfish mind plus another creates
an absurd confusion:
       Darkness then increases, and the good path
       is lost from sight.

✶ V.9 ✶

Immersed in the reality of the present moment,
the lover is above both belief and non-belief.
Love is the kernel of knowledge,
while belief and non-belief are both skin deep.

★ V.10 ★

Go beyond names and symbols. Look into qualities,
for good qualities lead you to your noble essence.

★ V.11 ★

Conflicts among people are caused
      by their attachments to words and names.
When they go into truth and meaning,
            peace and calmness prevail.

★ V.12 ★

Within you are present the bloodshed and conflicts
of all religions and nations of the world; beware that
one day you do not become a tool for one of them.

★ V.13 ★

You are essentially consciousness;
the rest of you is just bones and muscles.

★ V.14 ★

You are pure consciousness.
The rest of you is a mask covering consciousness.
Don't lose yourself; don't strive in vain.

★ V.15 ★

The human being is essentially vision;
the rest of him is just skin.
And vision is the real eye that sees the Beloved.

⋆ V.16 ⋆

Since I am a high-flying bird in the sky,
how can the flies of trivial worries reach me?

⋆ V.17 ⋆

Every day, from moment to moment,
a thought comes into your heart.
Regard each one of them,
like a dear guest visiting you, because
a person is valued and loved
on the account of his thoughts.

⋆ V.18 ⋆

Form comes from formlessness and
>*returns to God again* (*Qurân*, II:156).

Therefore, each moment you die and
>come back again.

⋆ V.19 ⋆

The Intellect is hidden, while
>this physical world has been made visible.

Our human forms are like waves and ripples
>coming from the ocean of the Intellect.

⋆ V.20 ⋆

Consider how every night all of our thoughts and
justifications are drowned in the sea of sleep,
but in the morning the Divine ideas, like fishes,
lift up their heads from the sea of serenity.

★ V.21 ★

Consider how in the autumn
hundreds of thousands of tree leaves and branches
    fall onto the land of death.
But each spring the Lord of the land issues an order
to the Emptiness:
> *Give back what you have consumed.*
> *Give back those plants, healing herbs,*
> *leaves, and grasses.*

From moment to moment, you too go through
    autumn and spring within you.
But look at the garden of your heart deep down:
It is green, watered, fresh, and full of
    rosebuds, cypresses, and jasmines.

VI. LOVE
June

If there is one key word – a single teaching – that sums up Rumi's work, it is Love (*eshg*). This word in its various expressions – separation, longing, pain, joy, beauty, union, spirit, and so on – runs like a common thread through the entirety of Rumi's poetry. Love is the alpha and omega of Rumi's school. His spiritual path is paved with love.

Love cannot be defined. Words fail to say what it is. Just as the taste of honey or milk cannot be put into words but must be tasted, love can only be experienced. Love is the force of creation and the alchemy of transformation. Love is what moves life, and the waves of love and life are embedded everywhere. Volumes of books and poems have been and will be written about love and its facets because the infinite love cannot be reduced to words, no matter how many.

Much like Jesus, Rumi views God essentially as Love. In fact, in his love poems, Rumi rarely mentions the word God; instead he says Beloved, Friend or the Soul of the souls. In this way, Rumi leaves the boundary between divine love and human love permeable because true love has the same source and essence of the divine, no matter how it is experienced or expressed.

⋆ VI.1 ⋆

Someone asked: What is love?
I said: You will *know* when you become like *me*.

Someone asked: What is love?
I said: You will know when *you* become *we*.

⋆ VI.2 ⋆

Whatsoever I say to describe love, when I come face to face with love I become ashamed of my own words. Although verbal expression elucidates the subject, pure love in action is more clear and brighter.

⋆ VI.3 ⋆

To love something that is merely flashy and fashionable is not true love; it ends up in failure, contempt and humiliation.

⋆ VI.4 ⋆

If the lover does not tell the mask from the face,
> he is the worshipper of the mask,
> not the lover of the beloved's face.

For the lover, the beloved is his daylight as well as his daily bread, his heart as well as his heart-burning.

⋆ VI.5 ⋆

Being a lover you may sway this way or that.
Nevertheless, being in love eventually leads you to
God.

✴ VI.6 ✴

A lover does not seek union
without being sought by the beloved as well.
When your heart is filled with the love of God,
rest assured God loves you too.

✴ VI.7 ✴

What you gain from a true religion is pure love, inner ecstasy, and the capability to receive the light of Divine truth.

✴ VI.8 ✴

The religion of love is separate from all religious institutions. The religion of lovers is communion with God.

✴ VI.9 ✴

Love is compassion and kindness without measure.
I say this because, in truth, love is a Divine quality
and characterizes His relation to creation.

✴ VI.10 ✴

Love has no affinity to this world or hereafter.
Love has its own world of frenzy and madness.

✴ VI.11 ✴

The lover is like a child drinking milk from the mother's breast. The child knows nothing in the world except *that* milk.

★ VI.12 ★

What is love? It is the ocean of nothingness.
The legs of intellectual reasoning become lame there.

★ VI.13 ★

Love results from inner knowing.
The ignorant of heart cannot sit on the throne of love.

★ VI.14 ★

Being a lover shows itself from the laments of
the heart. No sickness is like heart-sickness.
The lover's illness is different from all other
illnesses. Love is the astrolabe of Divine mysteries.

★ VI.15 ★

The love of the beloved brightens her cheeks with a
smile; the love of the lover consumes his soul in the
flames of love.

★ VI.16 ★

It is Divine wisdom written in decree and destiny
that we have been made lovers of one another.
All parts of this universe have been created in pairs,
and each one falls in love with a mate.

★ VI.17 ★

Love flowing through the soul and eyes of a living
person is each moment fresher than a rose bud.

✶ VI.18 ✶

Through love	bitterness becomes sweet.
Through love	copper turns into gold.
Through love	dregs taste like pure wine.
Through love	pains are healed.
Through love	the dead are made living.
Through love	kings become servants.

✶ VI.19 ✶

Without the care and attention of love,
the lover is like a bird without wings.
How can the lover have a sense of what is
before and after him if the beloved's light
does not illumine the path?

✶ VI.20 ✶

My sweetheart, the one I sought all my life, is here with me. My soul is grateful for this shower of grace and mercy.

✶ VI.21 ✶

Your body desires water and vegetables because
these things are its immediate origin.
Your soul desires spiritual life because
it is rooted in the Soul of Life
                            beyond space and time.

VII. Happiness
July

Life, liberty and the pursuit of happiness are featured as three cardinal human rights in the eighteenth-century United Sates' Declaration of Independence. What is happiness? Happiness has three levels or layers. On the most apparent and skin-deep layer, happiness is a sensory pleasure which is momentary, and depends on an external factor. On the second layer, happiness and sadness are two sides of the same coin. If what makes us happy is removed, we are then filled with sadness. Here again there is duality and attachment. On the deepest level, happiness is a state of consciousness, presence, bliss and heart-felt prosperity that result in a totally different attitude toward life and the world. We need and experience all these levels of happiness. But blessed are those who have reached the innermost happiness. Although even they experience pain, sorrow and grief, their innermost core remains detached, positive, peaceful, creative, strong, and compassionate toward everyone including themselves. In this chapter, Rumi's words take us on a journey of happiness.

★ VII.1 ★

A man asked Jesus Christ:
"What is the hardest thing to bear?"
Jesus answered: "God's anger!
    Because even hell trembles from it."
"How can one be safe from God's anger?"
"When you abandon your own anger," said Jesus.

★ VII.2 ★

You are veiled from reality because you have not realized the spiritual law of "Die before you die."
Unless the selfish ego dies,
    the sufferings of life will not end.

★ VII.3 ★

We collect corn in the barn,
but go on losing it because the mouse
has made a hole into our barn and
its mischief ruins our storage.
First avert the mayhem that the mouse can cause,
then work diligently to garner the corn for your soul.

★ VII.4 ★

The external fire can be extinguished by water,
but the fire of lust burns you all the way to hell.
What extinguishes this fire? God's illumination.

⋆ VII.5 ⋆

If you want suffering in your life to vanish, try to lighten up your mind. The mind produced by your carnal sense, fantasy and rationalization is devoid of the grace and light of the Glorious God.
Worldly knowledge simply increases your doubts and intensifies your illusions, while spiritual wisdom elevates you high above the wheel of this world.

⋆ VII.6 ⋆

At night when there is no light we don't see colors.
Therefore, we know light by its opposite – darkness.
                    To see light is to see colors.
But you know this for certain because
you have also seen darkness and "no colors."
Hardship and sorrows exist for this very reason:
        That the joy of the heart is manifested.

⋆ VII.7 ⋆

If a sad thought is blocking your road of happiness, it may as well be making preparations for your happiness. It powerfully sweeps dirt and dust from your house so that new joy from the benevolent source can enter.

⋆ VII.8 ⋆

Whatever sorrow shakes down or takes away from your heart, God grows better things in its place.
                                Be open.

✶ VII.9 ✶

All prophets have said: *Despair is not good*.
This is because the grace and mercy
   of the Almighty are infinite.
Beyond despair lie many hopes.
Beyond darkness shine numerous suns.

✶ VII.10 ✶

Where pain is, medicine goes there.

✶ VII.11 ✶

The usefulness of everything lies in its hidden
quality, as the cure is latent in the medicine.

✶ VII.12 ✶

Even a person as rigid as a stone in communion with
a person, who lives in the heart, turns into a jewel.

✶ VII.13 ✶

If you give bread for God's sake,
  bread will be given to you in return.
If you devote your life,
     life will be given to you.

✶ VII.14 ✶

When you see the flowing river of life,
   insert your jug into its water;
for water never runs away from the river.
When your jug is immersed in the river,
   you merge and become the river itself.

⋆ VII.15 ⋆

The Sufi is the child of the present moment.
To say "tomorrow, tomorrow"
      is not the hallmark of the Sufi path.

⋆ VII.16 ⋆

You should not feel lonely, my friend.
You are the whirling universe and a deep ocean.

⋆ VII.17 ⋆

The green garden of love has no bounds.
In it grows every kind of fruit except those of
           sorrow and happiness.
For being a lover is a state above
           sorrow and happiness.
Love is ever green and always fresh, with no spring
or autumn as such.

⋆ VII.18 ⋆

Every walker on the path of life, good or bad,
is dragged tight-handed toward God.
All people walk on this path,
bound in chains and full of fear and suffering,
except the friends of God, who are aware of the
secrets of God's action and creation.
Let your inner light shine and illuminate
so that your journey and work in this life
are eased and relaxed.

✶ VII.19 ✶

If the heart becomes the resting place of your
secrets, what you seek will be gained sooner.
The Prophet said:
> *Whoever enshrines his innermost thought,*
> *attains union with that object of desire quickly.*

This is because when seeds are concealed in the soil,
their secrets are revealed in
> the greenery and flowers of the garden.

If gold and silver were not concealed,
how could they grow in
> the mine and heart of the earth?

✶ VII.20 ✶

These physical eyes are the shadow of the spiritual
eye. Whatever that eye rejoices to see,
> let your eyes turn to it.

✶ VII.21 ✶

Everybody is terrified by death,
except the friends of God who laugh at death,
for their hearts are not conquered by the idea of
death: They know that
> what strikes the shell
>> does not destroy the pearl.

VIII. Heart
August

Heart (*del* or *galb*) is a recurring theme in Rumi's poetry and has a central position in his vision and teachings. Heart is the most vital organ in human's spiritual physiology. It is not merely an abode of emotions and feelings; it is a faculty of inner knowing, joy and love; it is the garden of the secrets of the Spirit. Although God's presence is everywhere, we can see this presence if we see God in our hearts first. Indeed, spiritual journey is none other than a journey to the heart, and spiritual life is none other than living through the heart. The heart is where we find the Spirit and comprehend the Secret. Thomas Merton once said, "This is a very important concept in the contemplative life, both in Sufism and in the Christian tradition. To develop a heart that knows God, not just a heart that loves God, but a heart that knows God. How does one know God in the heart? By praying in the heart." So let's read these short sayings of Rumi as prayers of the heart; these quotes are about the various stages of a journey to the heart and various facets of a journey through the heart.

✶ VIII.1 ✶

The fire of anger cannot be extinguished
    save by the light of the heart.

✶ VIII.2 ✶

The heart immersed in the tank of the body
    eventually becomes muddy.
The body swimming in the pond of the heart
    stays fresh and pure.

✶ VIII.3 ✶

The body is not concealed from the soul,
nor is the soul concealed from the body.
However, nobody – no body –
                      is permitted to see the soul.

✶ VIII.4 ✶

Little by little, life takes away physical beauty.
Little by little, the young tree withers.
Go and read this verse:
*To whomever we bestow a longer span of life, we
also give him declining health* (*Qurân*, XXXVI: 68).
Therefore, seek the heart.
Don't set your life's desire on bones,
for the beauty of the heart is the everlasting beauty.
The lips of the heart are drunken from
                              the Water of Life.

★ VIII.5 ★

Do you know why the mirror of your heart does not shine and reflect? Because the rust has not been cleaned from its face.

★ VIII.6 ★

Each person sees the Hidden Realm to the degree that his heart is polished and luminous.

★ VIII.7 ★

The Sufis polish their chests through meditation and remembrance of God. Therefore, their heart mirrors receive and reflect fresh images from the Source.

★ VIII.8 ★

The Sufis polish their chests clean from
> greed, desire, meanness, and hatred.

The heart is, indeed, a pure mirror,
> for it is receptive of infinite images.

The Sufis, in their chests, hold the pure mirror of the heart that reflects the infinite images from the
> Unseen Realm.

★ VIII.9 ★

Those who purify their hearts are liberated from the smell and color of materialistic life.
Therefore, each moment they witness beauty and goodness all around.

✶ VIII.10 ✶

When the heart's mirror becomes clear and pure,
you will see images
>from beyond the realm of water and soil.
You will see
both the image and the image-maker,
both the precious carpet and the one
who unfolds the carpet under your feet.

✶ VIII.11 ✶

The Book of the Sufi is not literal knowledge or
words. It is the heart as white as snow.

✶ VIII.12 ✶

Remember this:
The heart's mirror has no bounds.
Therefore, the limited intellect must remain
silent here, or else, it will mislead us.
For the heart is with God, or God is the heart.

✶ VIII.13 ✶

The heart is where the Divine light shines,
and it is beyond space and time.
How can time – past, future or even present –
dwell in the heart?

✶ VIII.14 ✶

The work which your heart desires to perform is also
where you can best manifest the glory of your talent.

★ VIII.15 ★

Prophet Muhammad said that God had revealed this to him:

*"I am not contained in any place –
above or below, on Earth or in Heaven,
not even on the Divine Throne.
Strangely, however, I am in the hearts of the
faithful. If you wish to search for me,
seek me in their hearts."*

★ VIII.16 ★

Certainly, there is a window from heart to heart.
Hearts are not apart or far from each other
    like two separate bodies.
Two lamps are not joined in body,
    but their light is mingled
        when the flame passes from one to another.
When the flash of Friend's love strikes a heart,
rest assured *that* heart is filled with love.

★ VIII.17 ★

No mirror becomes opaque iron again.
No bread becomes wheat again.
No ripened grape becomes sour again.
No sweet fruit is burned in the stove.
Become the ripened fruit,
so that you are free from becoming less.
Be an actualized human; become Light.

✦ VIII.18 ✦

The intimacy of the soil with rainwater
yields delicious fruits, healing herbs, and greenery.
The intimacy of a human with greenery
yields delight, happiness, and serenity.
The intimacy of life with serenity
yields goodwill, generosity, and kindness.

✦ VIII.19 ✦

What God says to the rose makes it smile.
What God says to my heart enriches and beautifies
me a hundred times more.

✦ VIII.20 ✦

Everyone can tell rebuke from kindness –
whether a learned, uneducated or a mean person.
But few people can recognize
      kindness hidden in rebuke, or
      vengeance in the kernel of mercy,
except the blessed one whose heart possesses a
yardstick of the human soul.

✦ VIII.21 ✦

A flower from whose heart sweet scent emanates,
indeed, reveals the secret of the flower.

IX. UNIVERSE
September

Universe means "one whole turning" – a single dynamic, interconnected world having the same source, foundation, and evolution. Today some scientists suggest that our universe may be one of the numerous universes. This notion of "multiverse" would not have surprised the mystic Rumi who often referred to thousands of worlds arising from an unseen realm. Multiverse does not explain away the origin of the physical existence; it simply multiplies the mystery and the majesty of the Source of all these. Our planet may be a speck of dust in the universe but the fact that we humans can think and talk about universes establishes a dignified and precious place for us in this evolutionary world – or God's creation if you prefer to call that. Contemplation on the universe is also a reflection on our lives and our consciousness in the world. This contemplation liberates us from the shackles, fears, illusions, and chores of the routine life. In his poetry Rumi paints a marvelous, grand, and glorious picture of the universe. But more importantly, Rumi's vision connects our perishable lives to the Grand Eternal. He once said, "In form, you are microcosm; in meaning, you are macrocosm" (*Masnavi*, IV: 521).

✶ IX.1 ✶

If the universe appears to you so vast and fathomless, know that the entire universe is smaller than a particle in the presence of Divine power.

✶ IX.2 ✶

This world is just a droplet from the River of God's beauty and love. And the world is here because of the River's overflow.

✶ IX.3 ✶

Each and every moment, you die and resurrect. The Prophet rightly said: *The world is this very hour*.

✶ IX.4 ✶

With each breath, we and the world are renewed again and again, but we are unaware of this, because the world maintains its appearance. Our life too keeps coming afresh each moment like a stream, although our body appears to be a continuum. Because the renewing process is so swift, each form looks the same as before. It is like when you whirl a firebrand swiftly with your hand, it appears to our sight as a complete ring of fire, but it is not.

✶ IX.5 ✶

Each and every moment caravan after caravan
come from the Realm of Emptiness
        into this World of Existence.

★ IX.6 ★

God does not give anything to anyone if there is no need for it. If the universe were not in need of the Earth, the Lord of the Universe would not have created the Earth. If the Earth were not in need of mountains, God would not have created these majestic features, either.

Therefore, everything comes into existence through a chain of needs. Humans too have been given tools and talents in proportion to their needs.

Elevate the quality of your need so that the bountiful sea of creation surges up in love and generosity.

★ IX.7 ★

Any plant that inclines upward
      is in a state of living and growing.
So it is with your soul:
When it inclines to a lofty state,
      it matures and grows to reach its heights.

★ IX.8 ★

The trees are like the dead buried in the earth,
but they have raised their hands and
make a hundred signs in order to speak
to those who have ears to listen.
With their green tongues and extended hands,
they reveal this secret of the earth's heart:
Although the green trees wither in the winter,
spring bestows them new life and greenery again.

✶ IX.9 ✶

The earth has the marks of God's patience and
generosity, for it takes manure and produces flowers.

✶ IX.10 ✶

The entire universe is a pitcher filled with the water
of life and brimming with intelligence and beauty.

✶ IX.11 ✶

From the intelligent works they perform,
you can know for certain that
the Earth and the Sky are intelligent beings.

✶ IX.12 ✶

A whole sun is hidden in each particle.
If the particle suddenly opens its mouth,
the earth and heavens will crumble to pieces
as the sun jumps out of the ambush.

✶ IX.13 ✶

Metals and stones are outwardly opaque,
but inside them lies the candlelight of this universe.

✶ IX.14 ✶

What is first in thought comes at the end of action.
Such was the foundation of the universe
                          at the beginning of time.
The fruit was the first thing in the seed's mind.
But in the process of creation it appears at the end.

★ IX.15 ★

To us, the names of things mean what they appear.
To the Creator, the name is its inner secret.
Consider, for instance, what we call "sperm."
In God's sight, the sperm means what you are now.
It existed in God's mind just as a full entity –
no more and no less. Now that "sperm"
has been realized as what is your name – human.

★ IX.16 ★

The fruit is the essence of a form we call blossom.
The blossom brings good news;

> the fruit is the reward.

But remember that the fruit appears
> only when the blossom is shed.

When the blossom disappears,
it becomes more than itself:

> The fruit grows in its place.

★ IX.17 ★

The creation of the universe is for the
manifestation of God so that the treasure of
His wisdom and love does not remain hidden.
God said: *I was a hidden treasure*.

> Listen to that!

Do not lose the gem of your being:

> Manifest it.

✶ IX.18 ✶

The origin of the Universal Workshop is
>non-existence, empty, and nameless.

That is why all masters, whether of crafts or of the heart, seek non-existence and emptiness
>in order to create and manifest their works.

Wherever this emptiness is in abundance,
>it is closer to God's Workshop.

✶ IX.19 ✶

See how the pen goes on writing,
>while the hand is hidden.

The horse is galloping;
>the rider is invisible.

The arrow is flying,
>but the bow is out of sight.

Countless lives are visible,
>while the Soul of all lives is concealed.

✶ IX.20 ✶

God has made the perishable world
>look like a grand existence.

And He has made the real existence
>look like no-thing.

He has covered the hidden sea with the visible foam, and has concealed the wind
>in what you see as the dust dancing in the air.

★ IX.21 ★

Wine in ferment craves our joy.
Heavens in motion beg our consciousness.
Wine owes its intoxication to us;
    we don't become drunk by wine.
The body owes its existence to us;
    we don't come from the body.
We are like bees, and our bodies are the honeycomb.
We have built this body, cell by cell,
    like the bee's wax.

X. UNION
October

One God as the alpha and omega of existence is the foundation of Islamic and other religious faiths. But this is not merely a philosophical argument or a metaphysical fantasy untouched by human life. Sufis believe that we all come from God, and unto God shall we all return (*Qurân*, II: 156). This returning to the Source is not merely an act of the after-life but a living principle of human thought and conduct. Union is a journey from separation to the beloved. And the human soul, at its deepest core, feels an existential separation, and thus longs for union, love, peace, and harmony. Union is also a vision of unity in multiplicity – that all beings are organically interconnected parts of a whole. Union is an appreciation of diversity for the greater good and beauty. Union is a sense of belonging to the deepest and greatest existence. Remembrance by the heart and walking on the path of love lead the seeker to the spiritual union in this very life. Science has made great strides in the intellectual understanding of unity in the multiplicity of nature, but the source of knowing and rejoicing union lies in the spirit and intuition; that is why every heart, in one way or another, yearns for love, union, and harmony.

✶ X.1 ✶

The realm of unity and union
                  is beyond the physical senses.

✶ X.2 ✶

Whatever you can think of is perishable.
That which cannot be contained in your thought
                                  is God.

✶ X.3 ✶

If you imagine that you have a "before" and "after,"
it simply shows that you are too attached to the body
and deprived of the life of spirit.
"Below," "above," "front" and "behind" are all
                  attributes of physical objects.
The nature of the illuminating spirit
                  has no such dimensions.
Open your inner eye to the pure light
                  of that majestic Being.
Then your thinking will not be short-sighted.

✶ X.4 ✶

Every person turns his face
          toward a certain side and direction,
except the friends of God who turn their faces
          beyond the sides and directions.

✶ X.5 ✶

Day and night appear to be opposites.
But they both weave the fabric of one reality.
Each, appreciating the other,
> goes on perfecting its own work
>> and complementing the other's.

✶ X.6 ✶

Life *is* when the opposites are in *harmony*.
Death is when they wage wars.

✶ X.7 ✶

The sea and the foam have different visions.
Pass the foam and see through the eye of the sea.

✶ X.8 ✶

How can we see the red, green, and brown colors without having seen them in light?
However, our senses become so attached to colors that a veil is drawn between us and the light.
When night falls and colors become invisible,
we realize that our vision of the colors was
> from the light itself.

✶ X.9 ✶

Hundreds of thousands of shadows,
> whether short or long,
dissolve into one in the presence of sunlight.

✶ X.10 ✶

Hidden things become apparent
> by means of their opposites.
Since God has no opposite,
> He remains unseen and hidden.
You perceive light by means of darkness.
Each pole reveals its opposite as it emerges.
The Light of God has no opposite
> in the entirety of existence.
Therefore, one cannot approach God
> through the duality of opposites.

✶ X.11 ✶

What is of the sea returns to the sea.
Whatever comes from a source
> eventually returns to that source.
From the mountain summit,
> the swift stream returns to the sea.
And within your body,
> the soul mingles with love.

✶ X.12 ✶

When 'I's and 'You's become one soul,
they all melt into the Beloved – the Soul of souls.

✶ X.13 ✶

Once we all were one essence –
> free and vast, without heads or legs.

We were one gem shining like the Sun –
> pure like water, without knots.

But when the pure light took form in creation,
it became multitudes,
> like the shadows of a battlement.

✶ X.14 ✶

All things perish except of the face of God.
> [*Qurân*, XXVIII: 88]

You can truly exist when you are
> in the presence of His Face.

Whenever your 'I' has died to love,
then *all things perish* is not your punishment.

✶ X.15 ✶

If in severe thirst you drink water from the cup,
> you will see God's Reality in the water.

But if you are not in love with God,
> you will see your own face.

✶ X.16 ✶

People try to climb the world
> on the ladder of 'I' and 'We.'

But eventually they fall down from this ladder.
The higher one climbs the ladder of selfishness,
> the more foolish he is,

for his bones will break more severely.

★ X.17 ★

If you look at the features of a face,
                              you will see two distinct eyes,
but if you look at the light of vision in the two eyes,
      the light is not differentiated.
Similarly, ten lamps in one place
is each different in form, but their light is one.
You may count a hundred apples,
                              each with juice inside,
but once you squeeze and blend them together,
there are no *one hundred apples*.
In the realm of meaning and spirituality
there are no divisions, numbers, or partitions.
Hold to the meanings and spirit of things;
attachment to images will deprive you of the Spirit.
Sweet indeed is the union of the Beloved
                              with His friends.

★ X.18 ★

When your soul is in union with God
and what is true and just, truth speaks through you,
and you will always see God in your mind.
This is because you are then emptied of your small
self and are filled with the love of the Beloved.
Remember: *A pot gives out what is in it.*

★ X.19 ★

Form comes into existence from the Formless,
                just as smoke is born from the fire.

★ X.20 ★

Although you are located in this place,
>   your origin is beyond space.
Do not chain yourself to this place;
>   be open to the Beyond.

★ X.21 ★

Listening to music is food for the soul of lovers,
because music carries a sense of union within.

XI. PRAYERS
November

s I write this note, there is a beautiful book of quotations from Mother Teresa on my desk. It is entitled, *Everything Starts from Prayer*. "I am asked," Mother Teresa says, "What is one to do to be sure one is following the way of salvation. I answer: Love God. And, above all, pray." Prayer is not a substitute for action; it rather strengthens our efforts and purifies our motives. Prayer is not in contradiction with the laws of nature and life; it is a spiritual part of them. Genuine prayer is rooted in a sense of gratitude, love, and a personal intimacy with God. That is why prayer has always been an essential practice in religions and spiritual traditions. Rumi was a man of faith and prayer; for him prayer was a love affair. In this chapter, we first read three quotes from Rumi about prayer and gratitude, and then several Rumi prayers from his poetry. I have selected only seven prayers – each to be used for three days. Prayers are words to be eaten, digested and become parts of our bodies and lives. Prayer brings out the best in us and radiates goodness in society. And as Ralph Waldo Emerson wrote in his *Essays*, "Prayer is the contemplation of the facts of life from the highest point of view."

✶ XI.1 ✶

A person of no prayer and no gratitude can easily be taken away by the wind of anger, lust, and greed.

✶ XI.2 ✶

Gratitude for your riches is
>   more delightful than the riches.

A person of thanksgiving and prayer
>   has no need to run after the riches.

Gratitude is the soul of the riches;
>   the riches are only the skin.

Because thanksgiving and prayer
>   lead you to the abode of the Beloved.

Riches, on their own, bring about
>   negligence of the Beloved,

while gratitude indicates mindfulness
>   and presence of the heart.

Therefore, enjoy the riches
>   in the Kingdom of God through gratitude.

✶ XI.3 ✶

Is there a closer way to approach God than prayer?
The answer is more prayer.
But prayer is not merely an outward form of words;
it is a state of total absorption and selflessness.

PRAYERS

★ XI.4 ★

O God, show me things as they really are
in this house of illusions.

★ XI.5 ★

O God, grant me such insight and discernment
that I can tell the false signs from the true ones.

★ XI.6 ★

Lord!
You are eternal, so is Your grace.
You are what I know and what I know not.
You have told us to remember You always,
for Your grace is always fresh and eternal.

XI.7

O God!
In this life, there are thousands of snares and baits,
and we are like poor greedy birds.
Although You created us like free brave falcons,
time and again we fall into a trap.
Each time, You liberate us,
but we move again into a new trap.
Even if there are thousands of snares on our path,
O Lord,
as long as You are with me,
I have no worries.

✶ XI.8 ✶

Lord!
Save us from our hands and
what they might do.
Lift the curtain before our sight,
but do not tear the curtain of our being.
Save us from the contaminated ego;
its knife has reached our bones.
Who but You, O Lord, and Your power
can break these heavy shackles on our feet?
Who but You, O Lord, and Your grace
can open this hard lock for us?
Lord!
Turn us from our ego toward Yourself.
You are indeed nearer to us than ourselves.
Even this prayer is Your teaching to us –
a gift from You.

★ XI.9 ★

Lord! You are the Spring,
and I am the green garden;
You are hidden, but
the bounty of Your Spring is everywhere.
Lord! You are the Spirit,
and I am like hands and feet;
You are hidden, but
these hands and feet move by You.
Lord! You are the Intellect,
and I am the tongue;
You are hidden, but
this tongue expresses Your Intellect.
Lord! You are Joy,
and I am laughter;
You are hidden, but
my laughter comes from your Joy.

★ XI.10 ★

Lord! Peace is You;
peace comes from You;
and onto You peace returns.
Lord! Grant us a life full of peace, and
let us enter Your abode of peace.
Lord! Your grace and blessings
come on the wings of peace.
O Lord of majesty and generosity,
all praise and glory belong to You.
Praise to You!
We have not been able to
worship You as ought to be.
Praise to You!
We have not been able to
appreciate You as ought to be,
although your presence is the most evident.

XII. Silence
December

We are approaching the end of our spiritual journey through the words of Rumi. We began with *Words* (chapter 1) and end here with *Silence*. Indeed, spiritual teachings and meditations should eventually lead us to silence. It is in the silence of the heart that we find God, joy, consciousness, love, union, and homecoming. No wonder why Rumi's Persian pen-name, which he used at the end of many of his lyric poems, was *khamoosh* – "Silence" or "Silent." So this is going to be a chapter on silence – a month of silence. You will review seven quotes from Rumi on silence (one for three days), and then go inward – beyond words into your own heart. After three days of no reading and inner silence, come back and write briefly the most impressive feeling and finding you experienced – condensed to a few lines. Now, these are your words arising from your heart on this spiritual journey. "Be still and know …" (*Psalm*, XXXXVI: 10). In *The House in Paris*, Elizabeth Bowen writes: "Silences have climaxes, when you have got to speak."

★ XII.1 ★

A human being is concealed beneath the tongue.
The tongue is a curtain over
the gate of the soul.

★ XII.2 ★

Our entire being consists in listening,
even when the physical ear is gone.
We are entirely speech,
even when our lips are closed.

⋆ XII.3 ⋆

The spiritual world is like the salt-mine:
Whatever goes there
loses its superficial color
and becomes pure.

⋆ XII.4 ⋆

No corner of this world
is without wild beasts or snares.
Only in the solitude of the heart and
the presence of truth
are you safe and peaceful.

★ XII.5 ★

The long night is meant for speaking your heart's
secrets and praying for your wishes without being
troubled by people – whether friends or foes.

★ XII.6 ★

At night, you attain solitude and peace,
and God lifts off your mask
so that your thoughts and deeds
are devoid of hypocrisy,
and full of purity and devotion.

✶ XII.7 ✶

When the candle is an entire flame
from head to foot,
shadow cannot surround it.
Through the flame of love,
the wax flees from its dark self
into the radiance of Him,
who fashioned the candle.
That radiance is eternal,
while the wax of your body eventually perishes.
The Divine flame and radiance resides
in the candle of your spirit.

RUMI'S PROVERBS

Proverbs are the treasury of practical and popular wisdom. Interestingly, some lines from Rumi's poems translated by Coleman Barks are frequently quoted in English, and have become almost English proverbs. For instance:

*Out beyond ideas of wrongdoing and rightdoing,
there is a field. I will meet you there.*

The vast majority of proverbs and oft-quoted phrases in the Persian language and culture come from the works of eminent Persian poets of classical times such as Ferdowsi, Omar Khayyam, Attar, Rumi, Sa'di, and Hafez. The Iranian scholar Ali Akbar Deh'khoda, who compiled the most comprehensive dictionary of proverbs and famed verses in Persian (entitled *Amsâl va Hekam*, "Proverbs and Aphorisms," in four volumes, 1931) lists 1260 verses from Rumi; this is almost five percent of the total proverbs in Deh'khoda's book. Here I have selected and translated 22 Rumi proverbs.

★ 1 ★

*Everyone became my friend
according to his own thinking.*

★ 2 ★

*An unripe person cannot understand
the state of a mature person.*

★ 3 ★

*A man had a donkey but no saddle;
when he got a saddle, the wolf took away the donkey.*

★ 4 ★

*We should pray to God to grant us
self-control and fine manners.
For whoever lacks these,
is also deprived of God's grace.*

★ 5 ★

*Being in love is evident
from the laments of the heart.*

★ 6 ★

*Sunshine is the proof of the Sun's existence.
If you want more proof, keep gazing at the Sun.*

★ 7 ★

*The Sufi is the child of the present moment.
To say "tomorrow, tomorrow"
is not the hallmark of the Sufi path.*

★ 8 ★

*Although verbal expression elucidates the subject of love,
pure love in action is more clear and brighter.*

★ 9 ★

[In expressing your love and devotion]
*Do not seek strict rules of conduct;
say whatever your home-sick heart desires.*

★ 10 ★

*It is more delightful to hear the secrets of love
narrated by others.*

★ 11 ★

*Water beneath the boat is its life support.
Water inside the boat is its death.*

★ 12 ★

*With each breath,
we and the world are regenerated fresh.*

★ 13 ★

Through love bitter things become sweet.

★ 14 ★

*Your friend's virtues are masked
when a grudge enters your mind.*

★ 15 ★

A human's character is hidden beneath his tongue.

★ 16 ★

You are essentially consciousness;
the rest of you is mere bones and muscles.

★ 17 ★

Don't seek water; seek thirst.

★ 18 ★

To be one in the heart is far better
than speaking the same language.

★ 19 ★

With children, speak in children's language.

★ 20 ★

Rigidity and prejudice come from
the immaturity of character.

★ 21 ★

A jar gives out what is in it.

★ 22 ★

One cannot drink the entire water of a river.
Only drink so much as to quench your thirst.

Rumi's Last Will

Rumi's biographer, Ahmad Aflâki, writing in the fourteenth century, reports that close to the end of Rumi's life, earthquakes hit Konya for seven days. Rumi, ever a mystic poet, said, "The poor earth is hungry and wants to consume me." He then gathered his friends and disciples, and gave the following advice to them. This is Rumi's Last Will:

I recommend you observe God
    both in the secrecy of your heart and
    in the visibility of the public.
Eat less and speak less.
Keep away from inhumane deeds.
Keep your practices of prayer and fasting.
Put aside egoistic desires and lust.
Be patient when people are rough with you.
Avoid the company of foolish and ignorant persons.
Maintain conversations with people of good deeds,
    generosity, and admirable character.
The best among people are those
    who serve others in useful ways.
The best words are brief and properly chosen.
Gratitude to God, the Only Reality!
Greetings to those who are one with the Reality.

THE REED FLUTE'S SONG

The entire 26,000 verses of the *Masnavi* were dictated by Rumi to his friend and disciple Husâm Chalabi over a period of twelve year, except for the first 18 verses which were hand written by Rumi himself. These 18 verses, popularly known as the reed's song, is probably the most famous poem of Rumi. The following is the first English translation of these verses by Sir William Jones, the founder of British Orientalism. This translation, first published in 1772, is in rhyming verse – a popular style in those days.

Hear, how yon reed in sadly pleasing tales
Departed bliss and present woe bewails!

'With me, from native banks untimely torn,
Love-warbling youths and soft-ey'd virgins mourn.

O! Let the heart, by fatal absence rent,
Feel what I sing, and bleed when I lament:

Who roams in exile from his parent bow'r,
Pants to return, and chides each ling'ring hour.

My notes, in circles of the grave and gay,
Have, hail'd the rising, cheer'd the closing day:

Each in my fond affections claim'd a part,
But none discern'd the secret of my heart.

What though my strains and sorrows flow combin'd!
Yet ears are slow, and carnal eyes are blind.

Free through each mortal form the spirits roll,
But sight avails not. Can we see the soul?

Such notes breath'd gently from yon vocal frame:
Breath'd said I? no; 'twas all enliv'ning flame.

'Tis love, that fills the reed with warmth divine;
'Tis love, that sparkles in the racy wine.

Me, plaintive wand'rer from my peerless maid,
The reed has fir'd, and all my soul betray'd

He gives the bane, and he with balsam cures;
Afflicts, yet soothes; impassions, yet allures.

Delightful pangs his am'rous tales prolong;
And Laili's frantick lover lives in song.

Not he, who reasons best, this wisdom knows:
Ears only drink what rapt'rous tongues disclose.

Nor fruitless deem the reed's heart-piercing pain:
See sweetness dropping from the parted cane.

Alternate hope and fear my days divide:
I courted Grief, and Anguish was my bride.

Flow on, sad stream of life! I smile secure:
Thou livest! Thou, the purest of the pure!

SOURCES AND NOTES

In selecting and translating this anthology of Rumi's quotes, I have used mainly his book of *Masnavi*, but also in a few places, his *Discourses*. The following is the full bibliography and citation.

M [*Masnavi*, pronounced *Mathnawi* in Arabic]

Masnavi-e Ma'navi ("Rhyming Couplets of Spiritual Meanings"), edited by Reynold Nicholson, Persian text, Amir Kabir Press, Tehran, 1957, reprinted numerous times. Reynold Nicholson also translated the entire book into English with commentaries: *The Mathnawi of Jalaluddin Rumi*, eight volumes (Luzac & Co., London, 1925-1940).

F [*Fihi mâ Fihi* or "Discourses"]

Ketâb-e Fihi mâ Fihi (The Book of "In It What Is In It"), edited by Badi al-Zaman Foruzân'far, Persian text, Amir Kabir Press, Tehran, 1969, and reprinted numerous times. Two complete English translations are available: *Discourses of Rumi* by A. J. Arberry (John Murray, London, 1961); *Signs of the Unseen: The Discourses of Jalaluddin Rumi* by W. M. Thackston (Threshold Books, Putney, VT, 1994; Shambhala, Boston, 1999).

Chapter 1. Words

I.1	*M*, I: 33
I.2	*M*, III: 3271
I.3	*M*, II: 1958-59
I.4	*M*, I: 1137-38
I.5	*M*, I: 296
I.6	*M*, I: 1060
I.7	*M*, II: 862
I.8	*M*, I: 515
I.9	*M*, I: 2379
I.10	*M*, I: 2383-84
I.11	*M*, I: 1027
I.12	*M*, I: 3279
I.13	*M*, I: 1627
I.14	*F*: 63
I.15	*F*: 19
I.16	*M*, I: 1061
I.17	*F*: 7
I.18	*F*: 7
I.19	*F*: 2
I.20	*M*, I: 2107-09
I.21	*M*, I: 1064

Chapter 2. Quest

II.1	*M*, I: 1-4
II.2	*M*, V: 4216-17
II.3	*M*, I: 1741
II.4	*M*, III: 4393-97
II.5	*M*, III: 3212
II.6	*M*, I: 3607
II.7	*M*, I: 822
II.8	*M*, III: 978
II.9	*M*, III: 979
II.10	*M*, I: 2504
II.11	*M*, V: 1733-35
II.12	*M*, I: 817-18
II.13	*M*, I: 820-21
II.14	*M*, I: 819
II.15	*M*, V: 4215
II.16	*M*, I: 303-04
II.17	*M*, I: 683
II.18	*M*, I: 1541-43
II.19	*M*, I: 3086
II.20	*M*, III: 4781
II.21	*M*, III: 4808

Chapter 3. Awakening

III.1	*M*, III: 2635
III.2	*M*, I: 409
III.3	*M*, I: 410
III.4	*M*, IV: 3632-33
III.5	*M*, I: 1329
III.6	*M*, III: 2655
III.7	*M*, IV: 1869-71
III.8	*M*, I: 987-88
III.9	*M*, II: 1280-81
III.10	*M*, I: 523]
III.11	*M*, III: 1272-73
III.12	*M*, I: 1124-26
III.13	*M*, I: 214-15
III.14	*M*, I: 1311
III.15	*M*, I: 1327
III.16	*M*, III: 2937
III.17	*M*, VI: 3526-27
III.18	*M*, I: 598-600
III.19	*M*, I: 600-02
III.20	*M*, II: 1292-93
III.21	*M*, III: 3364

Chapter 4. Life

IV.1	*M*, II: 810
IV.2	*M*, I: 982-83
IV.3	*M*, I: 984-85
IV.4	*M*, III: 1297
IV.5	*M*, III: 166
IV.6	*M*, I: 815-17
IV.7	*M*, III: 3472
IV.8	*M*, II: 274
IV.9	*M*, VI: 4657
IV.10	*M*, II: 881-82
IV.11	*M*, I: 1322
IV.12	*M*, II: 1272
IV.13	*M*, III: 2632-33

IV.14	M, I: 2296	VI.4	M, VI: 4044-46
IV.15	M, III: 128-29	VI.5	M, I: 111
IV.16	M, III: 203	VI.6	M, III: 4395
IV.17	M, I: 1078-09	VI.7	M, II: 2601
IV.18	M, I: 2201-02	VI.8	M, II: 1770
IV.19	M, III: 1618	VI.9	M, II: Prologue
IV.20	M, II: 1269	VI.10	M, III: 4721
IV.21	M, IV: 1201	VI.11	M, VI: 4047-8
		VI.12	M, III: 4723
		VI.13	M, II: 1532

Chapter 5. Mind

		VI.14	M, I: 109-10
V.1	M, II: 3559	VI.15	M, III: 4446
V.2	M, I: 2128	VI.16	M, III: 4400-01
V.3	M, III: 1511	VI.17	M, I: 218
V.4	M, III: 3038	VI.18	M, II: 1529-31
V.5	M, III: 2648-49	VI.19	M, I: 31-32
V.6	M, II: 278	VI.20	M, III: 2934
V.7	M, I: 334	VI.21	M, III: 4436-37
V.8	M, II: 26-27		
V.9	M, IV: 3280-81		
V.10	M, II: 3679	*Chapter 5. Happiness*	
V.11	M, II: 3680		
V.12	M, I: 3288	VII.1.	M, IV: 113-15
V.13	M, II: 277	VII.2.	M, VI: 721-22
V.14	M, IV: 3611	VII.3.	M, I, 377-380
V.15	M, I: 1406	VII.4.	M, I: 3698, 3701
V.16	M, II: 3561	VII.5.	M, II: 3201-03
V.17	M, V: 3676-77	VII.6.	M, I: 1128-1130
V.18	M, I: 1141-43	VII.7.	M, V: 3678-79
V.19	M, I: 1112	VII.8.	M, V: 3683
V.20	M, I: 1890-91	VII.9.	M, III: 2922, 2925
V.21	M, I: 1892-99	VII.10	M, III: 3210
		VII.11	M, IV: 2880
		VII.12	M, I: 722

Chapter 6. Love

		VII.13	M, I: 2236
		VII.14	M, III: 3913-14
VI.1	M, II: Prologue	VII.15	M, I: 134
VI.2	M, I: 112-114	VII.16	M, III: 1302
VI.3	M, I: 205	VII.17	M, I: 1793-94

VII.18	M, III: 4581-83	IX.7	M, II: 1812-14
VII.19	M, I: 175-78	IX.8	M, I: 2014-16, 2019
VII.20	M, II: 611	IX.9	M, II: 1803
VII.21	M, I: 3495-96	IX.10	M, I: 2860
		IX.11	M, III: 4411
		IX.12	M, VI: 4580-81

8. Heart

		IX.13	M, VI: 3579
		IX.14	M, II: 970-971
VIII.1	M, III: 3481	IX.15	M, I: 1239-44
VIII.2	M, II: 1369	IX.16	M, I: 2930-31.
VIII.3	M, I: 8	IX.17	M, IV: 3028-9
VIII.4	M, II: 714-716	IX.18	M, VI: 1467-70
VIII.5	M, I: 34	IX.19	M, II: 1303-04
VIII.6	M, IV: 2909	IX.20	M, V: 1026-27
VIII.7	M, I: 3154	IX.21	M, I; 1811-13.
VIII.8	M, I, 3484-89		
VIII.9	M, I: 3492		
VIII.10	M, II: 72-73	## 10. Union	
VIII.11	M, II: 159		
VIII.12	M, I: 3484-89	X.1	M, I: 3099
VIII.13	M, III: 1151	X.2	M, II: 3108
VIII.14	M, I: 635	X.3	M, I: 2007-09
VIII.15	M, I: 2652-54	X.4	M, V: 350
VIII.16	M, III: 4391-99	X.5	M, III: 4418
VIII.17	M, II: 1317-1319	X.6	M, I: 1293
VIII.18	M, II: 1094-96	X.7	M, III: 1258
VIII.19	M, III: 4129	X.8	M, 1121-22
VIII.20	M, III: 1506-08	X.9	M, VI: 1863
VIII.21	M, I: 2022	X.10	M, I: 1131-35
		X.11	M, I: 767-68
		X.12	M, I: 1788
		X.13	M, I: 686-88
## 9. Universe		X.14	M, I: 3052-53
		X.15	M, VI: 3643-44
IX.1	M, I: 524	X.16	M, IV: 2763-64
IX.2	M, I: 2861	X.17	M, I: 676-683
IX.3	M, I: 1143	X.18	M, VI: 4040-41
IX.4	M, I: 1144-46	X.19	M, VI: 3712
IX.5	M, I: 1889	X.20	M, II: 612
IX.6	M, II: 3271-3280		

X.21	*M*, IV: 742	8	*M*, I: 113
		9	*M*, II: 1784
		10	*M*, II: 136
11. Prayers		11	*M*, II: 985
		12	*M*, II: 1144
XI.1	*M*, I: 3796	13	*M*, II: 1529
XI.2	*M*, III: 2895-97	14	*M*, II: 334
XI.3	*F*: 3	15	*M*, II: 845
XI.4	*M*, V: 1765	16	*M*, II: 277
XI.5	*M*, III: 331-32	17	*M*, III: 3212
XI.6	*M*, I: 2633	18	*M*, I: 1207
XI.7	*M*, I: 374-76	19	*M*, IV: 2577
XI.8	*M*, II: 2444-49	20	*M*, III: 1297
XI.9	*M*, V: 3312-15	21	*M*, VI: 4041
XI.10	*Awrâd*: 1	22	*M*, VI: 66

12. Silence

Rumi's Last Will

XII.1	*M*, II: 845
XII.2	*M*, VI: 3526-29
XII.3	*M*, VI: 1857
XII.4	*M*, II: 591
XII.5	*F*: 13
XII.6	*F*: 13
XII.7	*M*, V: 674, 675, 681

Ahmad Aflâki (d. 1356 AD), *Manâgib ul-Ârefîn* ["The Acts of the Mystics"], Persian text, edited by Tahsin Yaziçi, two volumes (Ankara, 1976 & 1980; reprinted in Tehran, 1983), 3: 574.

Rumi's Proverbs

1	*M*, I: 6
2	*M*, I: 18
3	*M*, I: 41
4	*M*, I: 78-79
5	*M*, I: 109
6	*M*, I: 116
7	*M*, I: 134

ACKNOWLEDGMENTS

Anyone translating Rumi's poetry is greatly indebted to the scholars who produced critical editions of Rumi's works from various manuscripts scattered in personal and public libraries in Iran, India, Turkey, Egypt, England and some other countries. Reynold Nicholson, Cambridge professor of Persian and Arabic literature, was a pioneer among these scholars. Over the years, I have benefited from Nicholson's edition of Rumi's *Masnavi*, from which this anthology has been largely selected. I have also consulted the *Masnavi* editions and commentaries published by Abdulbâki Gölpinârli, Mohammad Este'lâmi, and Karim Zamâni. The *Masnavi* has been a three-decade exploration for me, and I am delighted to be a student of this spiritual and literary masterpiece.

The draft of this book was first read by three dear friends: Florin Nielsen, Teresa May Habibian, and Marie English. I am very grateful for their critical edits and generous suggestions; nevertheless, I alone am responsible for any possible error in the final version.

ABOUT THIS BOOK

The Words of Rumi: Celebrating a Year of Inspiration is an anthology of aphorisms, mainly collected from the six-volume book of the *Masnavi* by the Persian Sufi poet Mawlânâ Jalâluddin Balkhi Rumi (1207-1273). The serif font used for the text of this book is Times New Roman, originally designed by Victor Lardent for the British newspaper *The Times* in 1931. Although no longer used by *The Times*, it is one of most popular typefaces in printing.

ABOUT THE TRANSLATOR

Rasoul Shams is director of the Rumi Poetry Club. His previous works include *Rumi: The Art of Loving* (2012) and *Rumi Essays: On the Life, Poetry, and Vision of the Greatest Persian Sufi Poet* (2016). He first learned of Rumi's poems in his Persian classes as a young boy growing up in Iran. The works of Rumi and other Persian poets have been his spiritual companions for over three decades. He has studied and lived in India, Japan, and the USA.

ABOUT THE PUBLISHER

Rumi Publications is an imprint of the Rumi Poetry Club, founded in 2007 on the occasion of the eight hundredth anniversary of Rumi's birth in order to foster literature and art that nourish the spiritual life and enrich our global culture. We celebrate inspirational words and perennial wisdom. For more information visit:

www.rumipoetryclub.com
www.facebook.com/rumipoetryclub

NOTES

NOTES

www.ingramcontent.com/pod-product-compliance
Lightning Source LLC
Chambersburg PA
CBHW020902020526
44112CB00052B/1205